P9-DNJ-862

—

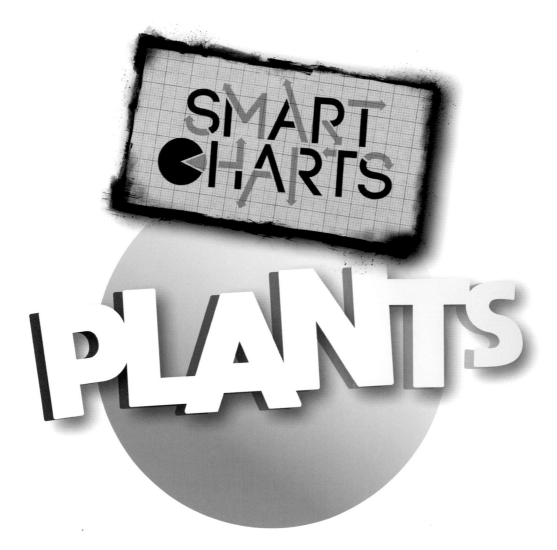

SMART CHARTS

PLANTS

By Madeline Tyler

BookLife
PUBLISHING

©2019
BookLife Publishing
King's Lynn
Norfolk PE30 4LS

All rights reserved.
Printed in Malaysia.

A catalogue record for this book is
available from the British Library.

ISBN: 978-1-78637-452-3

Written by:
Madeline Tyler

Edited by:
Kirsty Holmes

Designed by:
Daniel Scase

All facts, statistics, web addresses
and URLs in this book were verified
as valid and accurate at time of
writing. No responsibility for any
changes to external websites or
references can be accepted by
either the author or publisher.

PHOTO CREDITS

Front Cover – Picsfive, Kuttelvaserova Stuchelova, gilotyna4, Usenko Oleksandr, cash1994, Smileus, Incomible, KsushaArt
2. Smileus, Kuttelvaserova Stuchelova. 3 –gilotyna4, KsushaArt. 5 – Ortis, Dewin ′ Indew. 6 – gilotyna, bestofgreenscreen, Man As Thep. 7 – gilotyna4, Emilio100, Carmian. 8 – gilotyna4, Ian 2010, KRAS_U. 9 – Hert Niks, JSOBHATIS16899, Scisetti Alfio, Alewiena_design, Sunward Art, valzan, DutchScenery. 10&11 – Sergio Schnitzler, knahthra. 12 – gilotyna4, Ian 2010, kzww. 13 – LAURA_VN, Protasov AN. 14 – MRS. SUCHARUT CHOUNYOO, tunejadez, kzww, nevodka, Vadarshop. 15 – YARUNIV Studio, Kilroy79, freesoulproduction, Olesya Vovk, karamvi, HardtIllustrations. 16 – Dmitry Chulov, Independent birds, Mares Lucian. 17 – Sebastian Knight, aleksandr4300, Sunward Art. 18 – karen roach. 19 – Triff, wizdata. 20 – Beskova Ekaterina, peiyang. 21 – terekhov igor, Avigator Thailand. 22 – ilonitta, Toltemara, lady-luck, Anton Foltin, Rosalba Matta-Machado, Creative Mood, Scisetti Alfio, pjhpix. 23 – Kynata. 24 – Judah Grubb, wikki, runLenarun, oticki. 25 –Jabberocky, canbedone, MSSA. 26 – Sky vectors, NotionPic. 27 – Natali Snailcat, peiyang. 28 – Usenko Oleksandr, D. Kucharski K. Kucharska, Nathalie03. 29 – Martina Nolte, Nadya_Art, PONGPIPAT.SRI. 30 – prpunn, puaypuay, HelloRF Zcool. Graph paper throughout: photocell. Autumn leaves throughout: cammep. All backgrounds: Pieter Beens. Images are courtesy of Shutterstock.com. With thanks to Getty Images, Thinkstock Photo and iStockphoto.

PLANTS

SMART CHARTS

Words that look like **THIS** are explained in the glossary on page 31.

KNOW YOUR CHARTS!

WHAT IS DATA?

Data is another word for information. Data can be facts, numbers, words, measurements or descriptions. For example, someone might collect data about the different types of houses along a street. They might record how many houses there are, what colour they are, and when they were built. Data can be hard to understand, or **INTERPRET**, especially if it's a long list of words or numbers. Putting the data into a chart or graph can make it easier to read. Different charts and graphs are used to show different types of data.

TABLES AND TALLY MARKS

Tables are used to write down data about different things. They are usually quite simple and have a few rows and columns. Tally marks are used to count things up. The tally marks can be recorded in a frequency table. This shows how many of each thing there is. Tally marks are drawn in sets of five to make them easier to count. You draw four lines and then the fifth one strikes through the others.

HOUSE COLOUR	TALLY	TOTAL
RED	‖‖ꞁ ꞁ	6
BLUE	ꞁꞁꞁ	3
GREEN	ꞁꞁ	2
BROWN	‖‖ꞁ ꞁꞁꞁ	8
YELLOW	ꞁ	1

PICTOGRAMS

You can use the data from a frequency table to make a pictogram. Pictograms show the same information but with pictures or symbols.

RED	⌂⌂⌂	6
BLUE	⌂ꞁ	3
GREEN	⌂	2
BROWN	⌂⌂⌂⌂	8
YELLOW	ꞁ	1
KEY: ⌂ =2		

BAR CHARTS

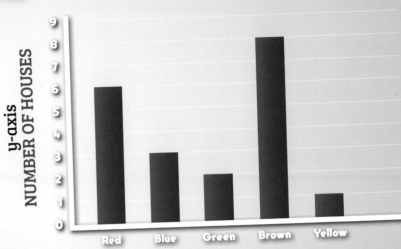

Bar charts usually show data that can easily be split into different groups, such as colours or months. You can easily compare the data in a bar chart and see which column is the highest.

Graphs have two axes. The one that goes up and down is the y-axis and the one that goes left to right is the x-axis.

PIE CHARTS

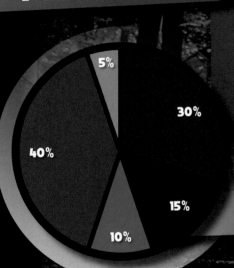

Pie charts are usually circular. They are split into different slices, just like a pie! Pie charts show data compared to the total number of something. For example, the total number of houses on the street is 20. Two of the houses are green – this is ten percent (10%) or one-tenth (1/10).

LINE GRAPHS

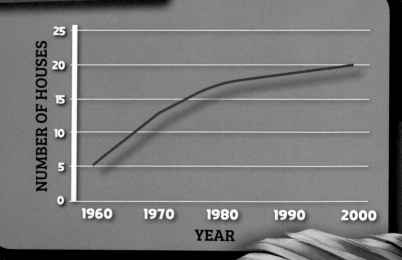

Line graphs show if there is a correlation (a connection or trend) between two sets of data. This line graph shows that there is a POSITIVE CORRELATION between the number of houses and time – the number of houses has increased as time has passed.

5

PLANTS

Plants are living things. They come in all sorts of shapes, sizes and even colours, and can grow almost anywhere on Earth, including underwater. Most plants have roots, a stem, and green leaves. Some plants have flowers and some produce seeds and fruit. Scientists **ESTIMATE** that there are around 400,000 different **SPECIES** of plants on Earth and these all have different features – every species is unique.

Plants are very useful and important for all life on Earth; they produce food and oxygen, which animals (including humans) need to survive. It would be almost impossible to survive on Earth if there were no plants.

TALLEST TREES IN THE WORLD

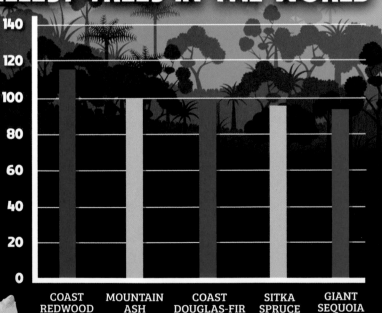

HEIGHT (M)

140
120
100
80
60
40
20
0

COAST REDWOOD | MOUNTAIN ASH | COAST DOUGLAS-FIR | SITKA SPRUCE | GIANT SEQUOIA

TREE

The tallest plant in the world is a type of tree called the coast redwood. One coast redwood, named Hyperion, was measured at around 115.7 metres (m) high. It's located in the Redwood National and State Parks in California, US.

PARTS OF A PLANT

Plants all have their own features that help them to live and grow. Most plants, such as trees, bushes and flowers, have common features including roots, a stem and leaves. These all help to keep the plant healthy. Fruit trees produce small flowers called blossom that eventually become the trees' fruit. All fruits, including apples, cherries and oranges, start off as flowers. Fruits can grow on large plants such as trees, on long, climbing vines, or on small shrubs and bushes.

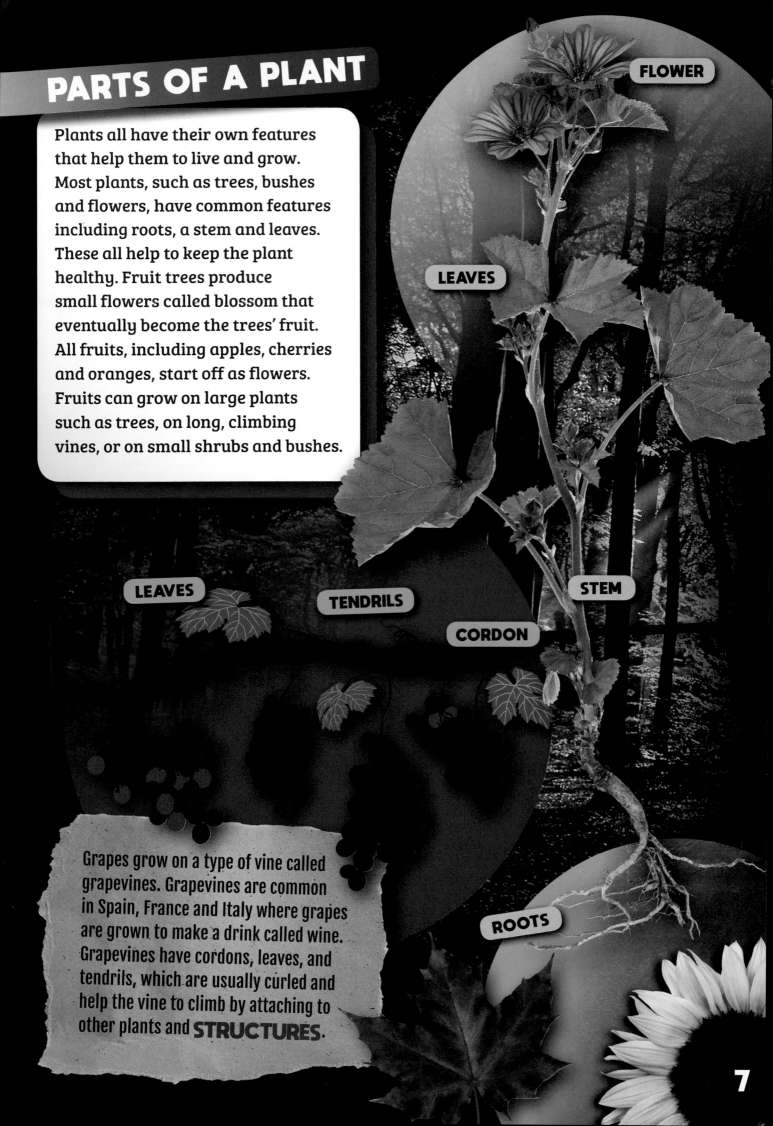

FLOWER

LEAVES

LEAVES

TENDRILS

CORDON

STEM

ROOTS

Grapes grow on a type of vine called grapevines. Grapevines are common in Spain, France and Italy where grapes are grown to make a drink called wine. Grapevines have cordons, leaves, and tendrils, which are usually curled and help the vine to climb by attaching to other plants and **STRUCTURES**.

7

FLOWERING PLANTS

Plants can be divided into two main groups: flowering plants and non-flowering plants. Flowering plants have roots, a stem, leaves and flowers, and produce fruit and seeds. Around 94% of all known plant species are believed to be flowering plants. This group includes most deciduous trees and every type of flower you can think of. Flowers are very important because they contain the things that a plant needs to produce fruit and seeds. They are usually very bright and colourful, and sometimes smell sweet too.

HOW MANY PLANT SPECIES PRODUCE FLOWERS?

There are a lot more flowering plants on Earth than there are non-flowering plants!

6%

94%

● FLOWERING PLANTS   ● NON-FLOWERING PLANTS

Deciduous trees are trees that lose all of their leaves for part of the year.

Non-flowering plants are slightly different; they don't have flowers. Instead, they are usually green and leafy, and release spores and seeds that they use to **REPRODUCE**. Non-flowering plants that use seeds to reproduce are called gymnosperms, and these include evergreen **CONIFEROUS** trees such as pines and firs. Some plants that release spores are mosses and ferns. Seeds and spores can be transported by the wind, flowing water, or animals.

Non-flowering plants look very different to the plants you might be used to. Lots of evergreen trees have very thin leaves called needles, and ferns have curly leaves called fronds.

Ferns are some of the oldest plants on Earth. The first ferns appeared over 300 million years ago and they can now be found all over the world.

PHOTOSYNTHESIS

Leaves trap sunlight. Plants can't photosynthesise without it! They also **ABSORB** carbon dioxide and release oxygen. Animals inhale (breathe in) oxygen and exhale (breathe out) carbon dioxide.

Glucose is made in a plant's leaves. It's carried from the leaves to other parts of the plant by the stem.

Like nearly all living things, plants need food, water, light and air to survive. Plants make their own food through a process called photosynthesis. The plant uses light and a gas called carbon dioxide to create a sugary food called glucose. The waste product left behind is oxygen.

Roots suck up water and **NUTRIENTS** from the soil. Nutrients are things that keep living things healthy and are needed for them to grow.

Water and nutrients are carried up the plant's stem. Water helps to keep the plant firm and stand upright.

SUNLIGHT

GLUCOSE + OXYGEN

CARBON DIOXIDE + WATER

Plants use sunlight to create glucose and oxygen from carbon dioxide and water.

WHEN DO PLANTS PHOTOSYNTHESISE?

0%

100%

● DAY ● NIGHT

Plants need sunlight to photosynthesise, so they can only do so during the day while the Sun is out.

PLANT REPRODUCTION

REPRODUCTIVE CYCLE OF A FLOWERING PLANT

1
Plants all usually have very similar life cycles. Most flowering plants begin as a small seed. If this seed finds its way underground, it can start to grow roots. A stem, leaves, and a flower **BUD** soon grow too. This is called germination.

2
Once the plant has grown taller, the flower will open. Pollen inside the flower is carried away by insects or the wind to other flowers. This is called pollination.

3
Pollen reaches a special part of the flower called the carpel. It travels to the ovary where it then **FERTILISES** cells, called ovules, to make seeds. This is called fertilisation.

4
The new seeds are spread by animals or the wind. This is called dispersal. Some of these seeds will land on the ground and may grow into new plants.

SEED → GERMINATION

DISPERSAL

POLLINATION

FERTILISATION

Some flowers grow a lot taller than others. The tallest sunflower ever grown reached 9.17 m!

HEIGHT (M)

10
9
8
7
6
5
4
3
2
1
0

TALLEST SUNFLOWER   AVERAGE SUNFLOWER

PARTS OF A FLOWER

Each part of a flower has a different job that helps the plant to reproduce. The stamen, which produces pollen, is the male part of the plant. The carpel, which contains the plant's ovary, is the female part of the plant. Some plants are either male or female and contain only a stamen or a carpel – these are called imperfect flowers. Other plants might contain both a stamen and a carpel – these are known as perfect flowers.

POLLINATION

For a plant to reproduce, pollen must be carried from the stamen to the ovary in the carpel. This could be in the same plant or between different plants. This is usually done by **POLLINATORS** such as birds, insects and some mammals. Many plants are pollinated by bees. In fact, around 80% of crops in the US are pollinated by bees.

HOW ARE CROPS IN THE US POLLINATED?

20%

80%

● POLLINATED BY BEES ● OTHER POLLINATORS

FERTILISATION

When pollen reaches the ovary, it fertilises the ovules. This produces new seeds from the ovules, while the ovary becomes the plant's fruit.

KIWI SEEDS

DISPERSAL

Once the seeds are ready, they are dispersed away from the plant. Some plants have seeds that are small and light and can be blown in the wind or attach to an animal's fur or feathers. Other plants have seeds inside the fruit. The fruit is eaten by an animal and the seeds then pass through the inside of the animal and are spread by their droppings.

WALNUTS

CHESTNUTS

Nuts and berries that contain seeds often taste good so that animals will eat them and spread the seeds. Some nuts, such as chestnuts, are fruits because they contain seeds, while walnuts are the seeds of the walnut tree's fruit.

FRUITS

Lots of flowering plants produce fruits. A fruit is the part of a plant that contains the seeds. Soft berries such as blueberries and cherries are fruits. Whereas some fruits, including hazelnuts and chestnuts are hard. Many things that you think are vegetables are probably also fruits. Tomatoes, cucumbers, avocados and pumpkins are all fruits because they have seeds inside.

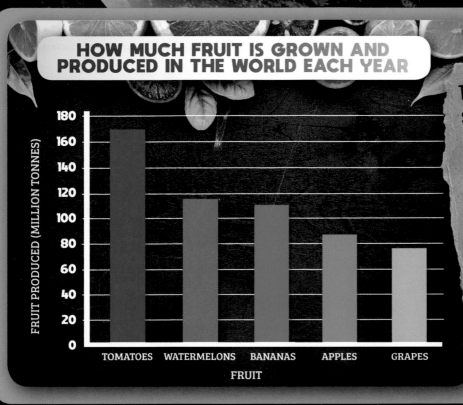

HOW MUCH FRUIT IS GROWN AND PRODUCED IN THE WORLD EACH YEAR

This bar chart shows some of the most popular and top-produced fruits in the world. How does this compare with the favourite fruits of people in your class at school? You could make a pictogram to see what the most popular fruit is.

TOMATO	🍅🍅
WATERMELON	🍉🍉🍉
BANANA	🍌🍌🍌🍌
APPLE	🍎🍎🍎🍎
GRAPE	🍇🍇

KEY: 🍅 =2

Does your pictogram look similar to this one?

REPRODUCTION IN NON-FLOWERING PLANTS

SEEDS

Some non-flowering plants produce seeds, but others produce spores. Conifer trees produce cones that contain everything the plant needs to reproduce. The cones usually look woody and are covered in lots of scales. Male cones produce pollen that is blown by the wind to ovules in the female cones. Just like in flowering plants, the pollen fertilises the ovules to produce seeds inside the scales of the female cone. Once they have **MATURED**, the fertilised female cones open up and spread apart their scales to disperse the seeds inside. The seeds can then grow into new conifer trees.

HOW DO CONIFEROUS TREES GROW?

HEIGHT (M) (vertical axis: 0, 2, 4, 6, 8, 10, 12, 14, 16)

YEARS PASSED (horizontal axis: 1 3 5 7 9 11 13 15 17 19 21 23 25 27 29 31 33 35 37 39 41 43 45 47 49)

Different coniferous trees grow at different speeds, and this can be anything from 15 centimetres (cm) a year to over 30 cm a year. Once a conifer tree reaches around 15 m, it usually slows down or stops growing.

Mosses and ferns don't produce seeds. Instead, they reproduce by releasing thousands of tiny spores. Spores grow on fern leaves and in moss, then fall off when they dry out. These spores are small and light, so they can be easily dispersed by the wind or by water. Sometimes, they might land on an animal's fur and can then be carried to new places when the animal moves around. If the spores land in a warm, **MOIST** area, they can start to grow into a new plant. Only a few spores land in the perfect place for growth, which is why these plants need to release so many. Plants that produce spores grow best in damp, shady areas like on the forest floor or under rocks and logs.

Mosses are very simple plants. They don't even have roots. Instead, they have tiny threads called rhizoids that hold the moss to where it's growing.

Unlike seeds, many spores contain both the male and the female parts of a plant.

TREES

LEAVES

BRANCHES

TRUNK

ROOTS

Trees are huge plants with one thick, wooden stem called a trunk. The trunk has to be very strong to support the growing tree, so it usually gets thicker as the tree gets taller. Most trees are covered in bark and have branches, leaves and roots. Trees are either deciduous or evergreen. Deciduous trees are flowering plants. They have wide, flat leaves that fall off every autumn and grow back in spring. Unlike deciduous trees, evergreen trees keep their leaves all year round. Coniferous trees are evergreen, and their needle-like leaves stay green in every season.

This line graph shows when deciduous trees lose their leaves, and when they grow back again. Can you see when deciduous trees have the most leaves?

LOTS OF LEAVES

AMOUNT OF LEAVES

NO LEAVES

SPRING SUMMER AUTUMN WINTER SPRING SUMMER AUTUMN WINTER SPRING SUMMER AUTUMN WINTER

SEASONS

TREE RINGS

Trees are some of the oldest living things on Earth – some are over 4,000 years old! Scientists work out how old a tree is by studying the rings inside its trunk. This is called dendrochronology (say: den-droh-cron-OL-oh-gee). Each ring represents one year of growth, so it's easy for scientists to count up the rings to see a tree's age.

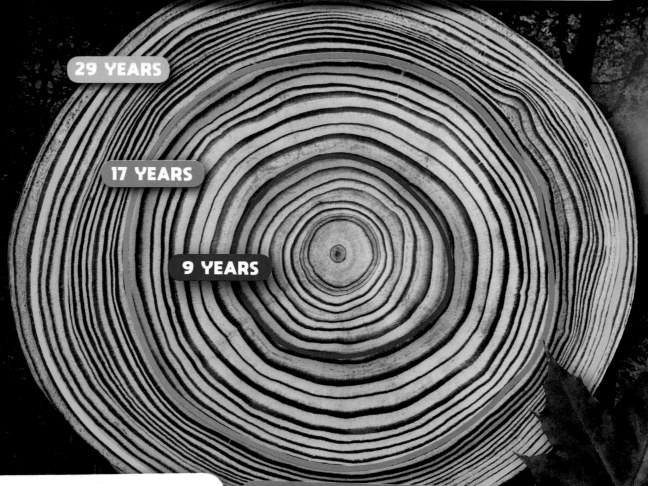

29 YEARS

17 YEARS

9 YEARS

Dendrochronology has allowed scientists to date some of the oldest trees in the world and calculate when they first started growing. The oldest-known tree on Earth is an unnamed Great Basin bristlecone pine in California, US. Scientists estimate that it is around 5,067 years old! This makes it around 500 years older than the Great Pyramid of Giza!

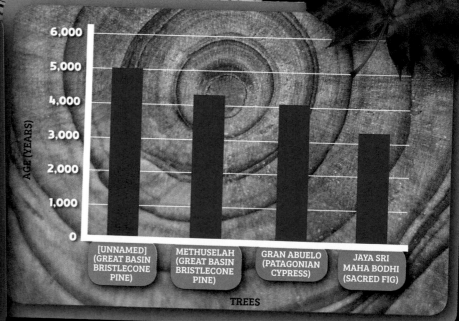

AGE (YEARS)

6,000
5,000
4,000
3,000
2,000
1,000
0

[UNNAMED] (GREAT BASIN BRISTLECONE PINE)
METHUSELAH (GREAT BASIN BRISTLECONE PINE)
GRAN ABUELO (PATAGONIAN CYPRESS)
JAYA SRI MAHA BODHI (SACRED FIG)

TREES

RAINFORESTS

When lots of trees and plants grow close to each other and cover a large area, it's called a forest. Forests can be found all over the world in hot, cold and TEMPERATE countries. Rainforests are a type of forest that receive a lot of rain and are usually warm all year round. Tropical rainforests are found near to the **EQUATOR** and are some of the most BIODIVERSE areas on Earth. They are home to lots of different plants and animals that can't be found anywhere else on the planet.

WHERE ARE EARTH'S SPECIES OF ANIMALS AND PLANTS FOUND?

50%

50%

● ELSEWHERE ON EARTH
● IN RAINFORESTS

HOW MUCH OF THE LAND ON EARTH IS COVERED IN RAINFORESTS

6%

94%

● RAINFORESTS
● OTHER

Rainforests cover around 6% of the land on Earth but are home to around half of all the plant and animal species on the planet!

THE AMAZON RAINFOREST

The Amazon rainforest is a rainforest in South America. It can be found in Brazil, Peru, Colombia, Venezuela, Ecuador, Bolivia, Guyana, French Guiana and Suriname. The Amazon rainforest is the largest tropical rainforest in the world and is very important for life on Earth. Lots of the food we eat and many of the medicines we rely on to make us better when we're ill were first discovered as plants in the Amazon rainforest. As well as this, the Amazon rainforest also helps us to breathe! It's sometimes referred to as the 'lungs of the planet' because it produces around 20% of all the world's oxygen. Sadly, huge areas of the Amazon rainforest are being cut down every day to make space to grow crops and for cows to **GRAZE**.

DEFORESTATION OF THE AMAZON RAINFOREST IN BRAZIL (1988-2017)

AMOUNT OF RAINFOREST LOST (SQUARE KM)

35000
30000
25000
20000
15000
10000
5000
0

1988 1989 1990 1991 1992 1993 1994 1995 1996 1997 1998 1999 2000 2001 2002 2003 2004 2005 2006 2007 2008 2009 2010 2011 2012 2013 2014 2015 2016 2017

YEARS

Many animals in the Amazon, like the macaw, are now in danger of becoming **EXTINCT** because so much of their **HABITAT** is being destroyed by deforestation.

21

CACTI

Plants in the rainforest grow best in a hot and wet **CLIMATE** with lots of rainfall, but some plants can survive in very dry conditions with almost no rain at all. Deserts are some of the driest places on Earth, receiving only around 400 millimetres (mm) of rain a year. When you think of a desert, you might imagine somewhere very hot and sandy, but deserts can be cold too.

Cacti are a type of plant found almost only in hot deserts in the Americas. Of the more than 2,000 species of cactus on Earth, only one – Rhipsalis baccifera, or mistletoe cactus – isn't **NATIVE** to the Americas. It grows across Africa as well as in Sri Lanka and Madagascar.

CACTUS

NATIVE TO AFRICA

SAGUARO

BARREL CACTUS

PRICKLY PEAR

ORGAN PIPE CACTUS

MISTLETOE CACTUS

SPIRAL ALOE

BAOBAB

JADE PLANT

Some plants are a type of cactus, and some plants are native to Africa, but only one plant is both of these things!

Cacti have many **ADAPTATIONS** that help them to survive in the desert and stay alive when there may not be much water available to them. Cacti have long roots that can spread out very wide to collect as much water from the ground as possible. Plants lose water from their leaves, so cacti have thin spines or needles to reduce the amount of water they lose. Some cacti don't have any leaves, spines or needles at all!

The saguaro is a tall cactus that grows in the Sonoran Desert in Arizona, US, and Sonora, Mexico. Once its roots have absorbed water from the soil, the saguaro can store the water in its thick, green stem. Some large saguaro cacti can store up to 1,000 kilograms (kg) of water!

How do cacti photosynthesise if they don't have leaves? Their green stems do the jobs that a plant's leaves would usually do! The stems absorb sunlight and carbon dioxide, release oxygen and produce glucose.

Producing flowers uses up a lot of water, so some cacti have flowers that only **BLOOM** at night. This helps the cactus to save water during the day when it's much warmer. It also means that **NOCTURNAL** animals such as bats and moths can pollinate the flowers.

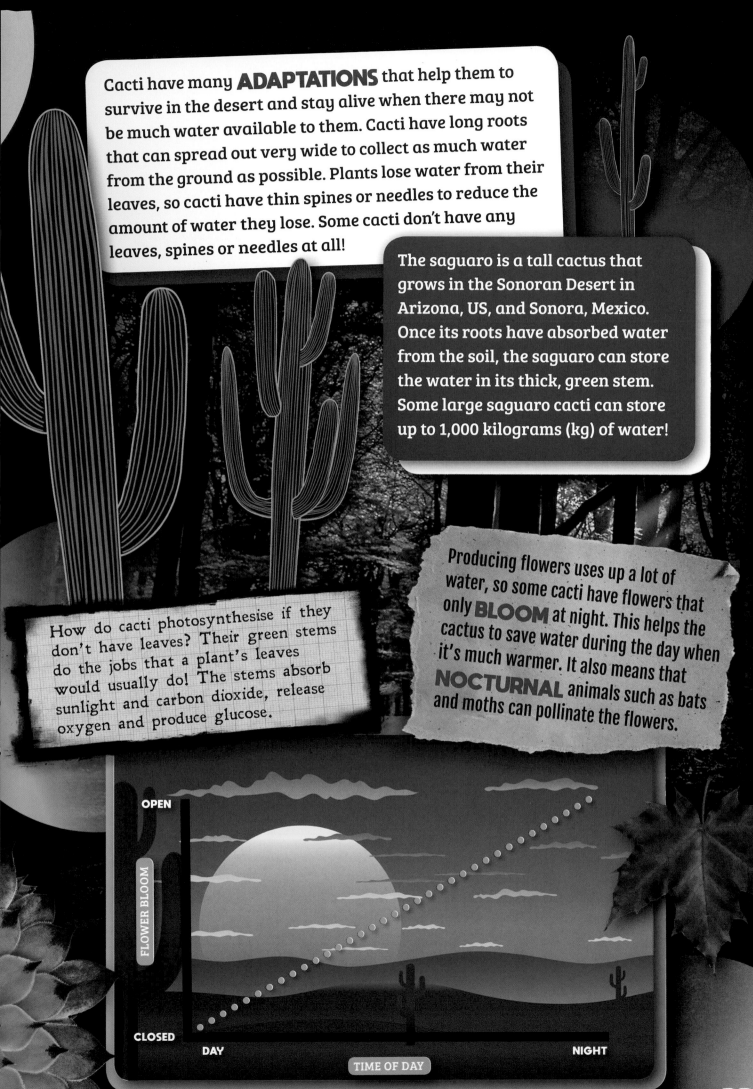

OPEN

FLOWER BLOOM

CLOSED

DAY

NIGHT

TIME OF DAY

CROPS

Lots of plants are grown all around the world to feed the animals and people on the planet. These plants are called crops. Some of the most important crops for producing food are maize, rice, oats and wheat, which are all cereals. Cereals are a type of grass that produce grains. Grains are seeds that can be ground up in mills to be made into flour. The flour can then be used to make things such as pasta and bread.

BEARD

HEAD

KERNEL

STEM

WHAT IS WHEAT USED FOR?

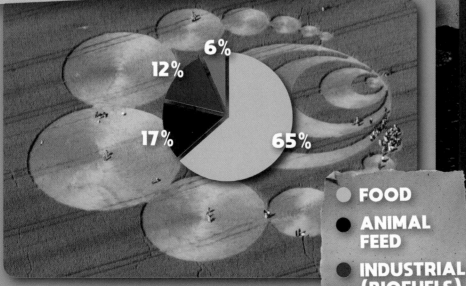

6%

12%

17%

65%

● FOOD

● ANIMAL FEED

● INDUSTRIAL (BIOFUELS)

● OTHER

One of the most-grown crops in the world is wheat. More of Earth is covered by wheat than by any other cereal or crop. Wheat is used to make flour which can be found in pasta, cakes, cookies and pastries.

Crops take up around 12% of all land on Earth that isn't covered in ice. This is a lot of space, which means that a lot of fields are needed to grow all of these crops. In fact, you've probably seen some of these fields before. Sometimes, strange **FORMATIONS** appear in crop fields overnight. These are called crop circles and they are usually made up of crops that are flattened in circular shapes to create a huge pattern. How and why crop circles are created is a mystery. Some people believe that aliens from outer space travel to Earth and leave messages for us in the circles, while other people think that strong winds and storms may flatten crops and leave the shapes in the fields.

HOW MUCH LAND ON EARTH IS USED FOR GROWING CROPS?

12%

88%

- CROPS
- OTHER LAND

UNDERWATER PLANTS

Plants don't just grow on land; they can also be found underwater in the ocean. Seagrasses are one of the most common types of plants found in the ocean. They have roots, stems and leaves, just like plants on land. They can be found all over the world and grow on the ocean floor to form large, underwater meadows. Animals such as dugongs, manatees and green turtles graze on the seagrass meadows.

The ocean is also full of many other living things that may look like and act like plants but aren't actually plants at all. One example of this is seaweed, which is a type of algae. Algae are a group of plant-like **ORGANISMS** that live in the water and photosynthesise. Seaweed doesn't have any roots, stems or leaves but, because it's an algae, it does photosynthesise.

OCEAN SURFACE 16	
15	
14	
13	
12	
11	
10	
HEIGHT (M) 9	
8	
7	
6	
5	
4	
3	
2	
1	
0	
SEABED	ZOSTERA CAULESCENS

Zostera caulescens is the tallest species of seagrass. It's found growing up to 16 m below the surface of the ocean and can grow up to 7 m long.

The ocean can be divided into three different light zones, or layers, depending on how much sunlight reaches each layer. The top 80 m of the ocean is called the sunlit or euphotic (say: you-FOH-tic) zone, and it receives the most sunlight. Plants need sunlight to photosynthesise, so most MARINE plants, including many seagrasses, are found in this zone.

Sunlight is made up of all the colours in the rainbow. The different colours of light can reach different depths. For example, red light can't reach much deeper than the ocean's surface, but blue light can reach around 200 m below the surface. Plants use different coloured light for different things during photosynthesis, and some plants under the sea photosynthesise by using only the light that can reach them: green, violet and blue.

HOW DEEP CAN LIGHT TRAVEL?

| RED | ORANGE | YELLOW | GREEN | BLUE | VIOLET |

OCEAN DEPTH (M)

0
50
100
150
200
250
300

EXTREME PLANTS

VENUS FLYTRAP

Venus flytraps grow in **BOGS** in North Carolina and South Carolina in the US. Just like other plants, Venus flytraps photosynthesise using sunlight, water and carbon dioxide. Plants usually absorb this water, and also important nutrients, from the soil using their roots. However, the soil that Venus flytraps grow in is very wet and doesn't have the nutrients that the plants need to survive. To help with this, Venus flytraps have **EVOLVED** to grow special leaves that trap and **DIGEST** insects that can give them the nutrients they need. The leaves are like sticky mouths with lots of sharp, spiky teeth around the edge. Insects land on the leaves because they produce a sweet liquid called nectar. The leaves' jaws then close on the insect in under a second and trap it there so it can't escape.

WHAT DO VENUS FLYTRAPS EAT?

Venus flytraps mostly eat ants and spiders, but they also eat beetles, grasshoppers, flies, and other insects.

- ANTS
- SPIDERS
- GRASSHOPPERS
- FLYING INSECTS
- BEETLES
- OTHER INSECTS

CASTOR OIL PLANT

Some plants aren't just dangerous to insects; they're also deadly to larger animals, including humans! When something is poisonous, it means that it could harm or kill the person or animal that eats it. Plants sometimes use poison to protect themselves from being killed and eaten by plant-eating animals. Many people believe that the castor oil plant is one of the most poisonous plants in the world. Its seeds, sometimes called beans, contain a poison called ricin, and just one bean contains enough to kill a human!

HOW MANY CASTOR BEANS DOES IT TAKE TO KILL DIFFERENT ANIMALS?

NUMBER OF BEANS

90
80
70
60
50
40
30
20
10
0

HUMAN   DOG   DUCK

Ducks and dogs may be much smaller than humans, but it actually takes more castor beans to harm them! Humans are much more sensitive to the ricin in castor beans than these animals are.

Lots of plants are deadly or poisonous, so you should never touch or eat anything that you're not sure of.

29

ACTIVITY: GET SMART!

DAY	SUNFLOWER HEIGHT (CM)
1	0
2	0
3	0
4	0
5	0
6	0
7	0
8	0
9	0.5
10	1
11	4
12	7
13	10
14	13
15	16

Plant a sunflower seed in a small plant pot and measure how much your new plant grows every day! Record your results in a table and use this to create a line graph. Make sure you remember to measure your sunflower every day!

Sunflowers need lots of sunlight to grow well, so make sure you keep your plant pot somewhere sunny. Remember to water it, too!

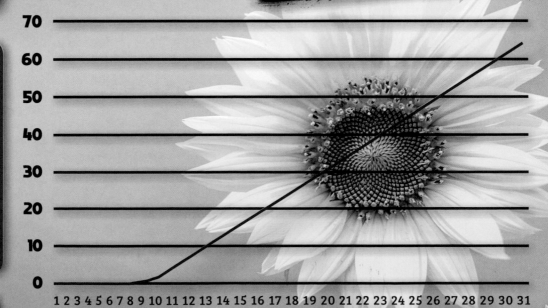

GLOSSARY

ABSORB — to take in or soak up

ADAPTATIONS — changes or characteristics that occur over time to suit different conditions

BIODIVERSE — when an area has lots of different types of animals or plants

BLOOM — when a flower bud opens

BOGS — areas of wet, muddy ground

BUD — a small growth on a plant that develops into a leaf, flower or shoot

CLIMATE — the common weather in a certain place

CONIFEROUS — relating to mostly evergreen trees and shrubs that have needle shaped or scale-like leaves

DIGEST — to break down food into things that can be absorbed and used

EQUATOR — the imaginary line around the Earth that is an equal distance from the North and South Poles

ESTIMATE — guess based on facts

EVOLVED — gradually developed over a long time

EXTINCT — when a species of animal is no longer alive

FERTILISES — to cause an egg to develop into a new living thing

FORMATIONS — patterns

GRAZE — eat grass in a field

HABITAT — the natural environment in which animals or plants live

INTERPRET — to understand or work out

MARINE — relating to the ocean

MATURED — grown fully

MOIST — slightly wet

NATIVE — of indigenous origin to

NOCTURNAL — active at night instead of during the day

NUTRIENTS — natural substances that plants and animals need to grow and stay healthy

ORGANISMS — individual plants or animals; individual living things

POLLINATORS — things that move pollen from one part of a plant to another, or between different plants

POSITIVE CORRELATION — a relationship between two sets of data where they increase or decrease together

REPRODUCE — to produce young

SPECIES — a group of very similar animals or plants that are capable of producing young together

STRUCTURES — buildings or other objects

TEMPERATE — a region or climate that is characterised by mild temperatures

INDEX